From Trash to Treasures

Cardboard

Daniel Nunn

Heinemann Library
Chicago, Illinois

www.heinemannraintree.com
Visit our website to find out more information about Heinemann-Raintree books.

To order:
☎ Phone 888-454-2279
🖥 Visit www.heinemannraintree.com
to browse our catalog and order online.

Edited by Rebecca Rissman, Daniel Nunn, and Sian Smith
Designed by Joanna Hinton-Malivoire
Picture research by Tracy Cummins
Originated by Capstone Global Library Ltd
Printed and bound in China by South China Printing Company Ltd

15 14 13 12 11
10 9 8 7 6 5 4 3 2 1

Library of Congress Cataloging-in-Publication Data
Nunn, Daniel.
  Cardboard / Daniel Nunn.—1.
     pages cm.—(From Trash to Treasures)
  Includes bibliographical references and index.
  ISBN 978-1-4329-5150-4 (hc)—ISBN 978-1-4329-5159-7 (pb) 1. Paper work—Juvenile literature. 2. Paperboard—Recycling—Juvenile literature. I. Title.
  TT870.N86 2011
  745.592—dc22   2010049822

Acknowledgments
We would like to thank the following for permission to reproduce photographs: Getty Images pp. 9 (James Hardy), 17 (Flying Colours Ltd); Heinemann Raintree pp. 6, 10, 11, 12, 13, 14, 15, 16, 18, 19, 20, 21, 23a, 23b, 23c, 23d, 23f (Karon Dubke); istockphoto pp. 7 (© Rob Hill), 8 (© Petr Nad), 22a (© Muammer Mujdat Uzel), 23e (© David Franklin); Shutterstock pp. 4 (© Shawn Hempel), 5 (© Stephen Coburn), 22b (© James M. Phelps, Jr.), 22c (© ID1974).

Cover photograph of cardboard animals reproduced with permission of Shutterstock (© holbox). Cover inset image of a box reproduced with permission of Shutterstock (johnnyscriv). Back cover photographs of a cardboard spider and a bird feeder reproduced with permission of Heinemann Raintree (Karon Dubke).

Every effort has been made to contact copyright holders of material reproduced in this book. Any omissions will be rectified in subsequent printings if notice is given to the publisher.

Contents

Some words are shown in bold, **like this**. You can find them in the glossary on page 23.

What Is Cardboard?

Cardboard is a **material** that is often used in **packaging**.

Cardboard is made of very thick paper.

When you buy something from a store, it often comes in a cardboard box.

Toys, eggs, and breakfast cereal can all come in kinds of cardboard packaging.

What Happens When You Throw Cardboard Away?

Cardboard is very useful.

But when you have finished with it, do you throw it away?

If so, then your cardboard will end up at a garbage dump.

It will be buried in the ground and may stay there for a very long time.

What Is Recycling?

It is much better to **recycle** cardboard instead of throwing it away.

Separate cardboard from your other trash and then put it in a recycling bin.

The cardboard will be collected and taken to a **factory**.

Then the cardboard will be made into something new.

How Can I Reuse Old Cardboard?

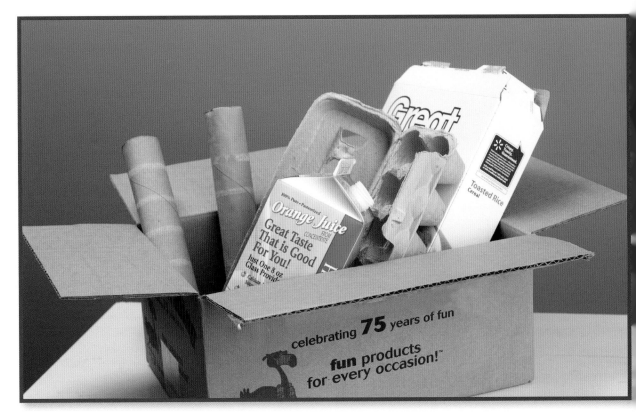

You can also use old cardboard to make your own new things.

When you have finished with a box or roll made of cardboard, put it somewhere safe.

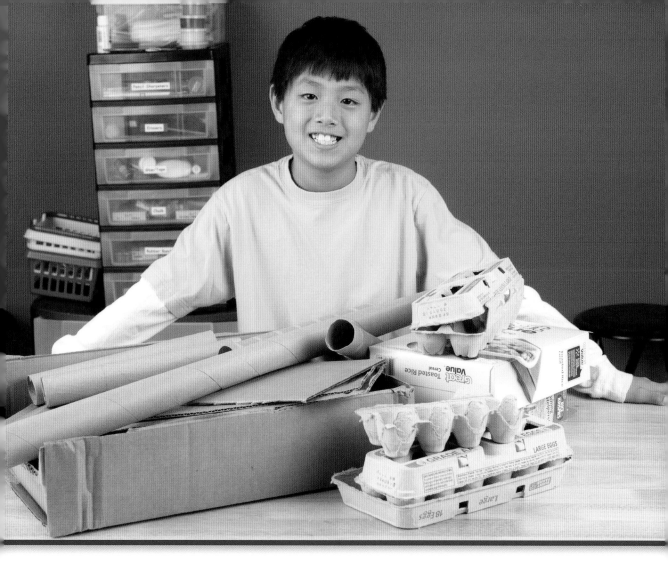

Soon you will have lots of cardboard waiting to be reused.

You are ready to turn your trash into treasures!

What Can I Make with Cardboard Rolls?

Cardboard rolls are used to hold paper towels, toilet paper, or wrapping paper.

But you can use them to make fun people puppets.

You can also use them to make your own musical instruments.

It is easy to make your own cardboard **kazoo**.

What Can I Make with Egg Cartons?

You can use an egg **carton** to make your own indoor garden.

You can plant seeds in each cup.

Egg cartons can also be made into great model insects.

This spider, caterpillar, and ladybug have all been made from one egg carton.

What Can I Make with Cardboard Boxes?

This milk **carton** has been made into a bird feeder.

You can use it to give food to birds all year long.

Large cardboard boxes can be made into almost anything.

This box has been made into a house!

Make Your Own Juice Box Boat

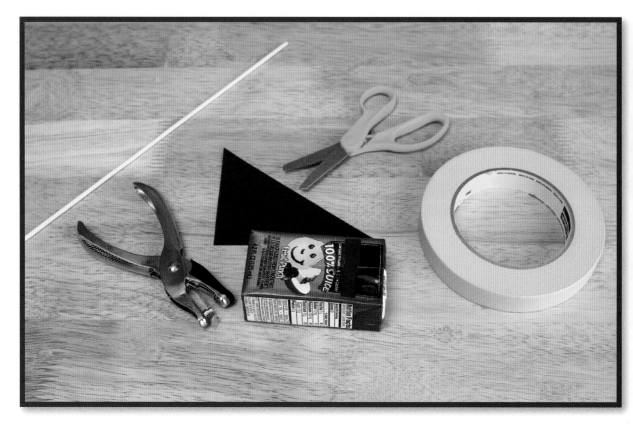

You can use an old juice box **carton** to make your own boat.

You will need an empty juice box carton, a stick, some cardboard, tape, scissors, and a hole punch.

First, cut a triangle out of the cardboard and use the hole punch to make a hole at the top and bottom.

Next, slip the stick through the two holes in the triangle.

Use the tape to cover the hole in the **carton** where the straw used to go.

Then use the stick to make a hole in the side of the carton.

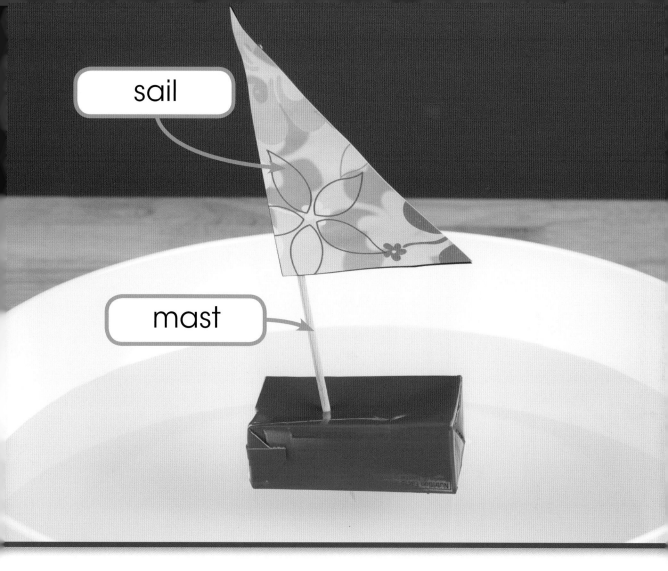

sail

mast

Push the stick through the hole in
the carton to make the sail and mast.

Decorate the boat and put it in water.
Blow on the sail to make your boat move!

Recycling Quiz

One of these photographs shows furniture made from **recycled** cardboard. Can you guess which one? (The answer is on page 24.)

Glossary

 **carton** small cardboard container. Some cartons are covered with a special material that helps them to hold liquids.

 **factory** building where something is made

 **kazoo** musical instrument that makes a buzzing sound when you hum into it

 **material** what something is made of

 **packaging** box or wrapping that something comes in

 **recycle** break down a material and use it again to make something new

Find Out More

Ask an adult to help you make fun things with cardboard using the websites below.

Animals: **www.enchantedlearning.com/crafts/ Eggcarton.shtml**

Bird feeder: **www.ziggityzoom.com/activities. php?a=302**
Kazoo: **www.makingfriends.com/music/kazoo.htm**

Puppets: **www.makingfriends.com/recycle/tp_ puppets.htm**

Seed garden: **www.freekidscrafts.com/seedling_ pot-e678.html**

Answer to question on page 22
The chair on the right is made from recycled cardboard.

Index